Laura Esquivel

Between Two Fires

INTIMATE WRITINGS ON LIFE, LOVE, FOOD & FLAVOR

Translated by Stephen Lytle

Crown Publishers

New York

Published by Crown Publishers, New York, New York.
Member of the Crown Publishing Group.

Random House, Inc. New York, Toronto, London, Sydney, Auckland
www.randomhouse.com.

CROWN is a trademark and the Crown colophon is a registered
trademark of Random House, Inc.

Originally published in Spanish by Ollero & Ramos, Editores,
S. L. (Madrid) in 1998. Copyright © 1998 by Laura Esquivel.

Printed in the United States of America.

Typographic design by Barbara Sturman

Library of Congress Cataloging-in-Publication Data
Esquivel, Laura, 1950–
    [Intimas suculencias. English]
    Between two fires : intimate writings on life, love, food and
    flavor / by Laura Esquivel ; translated by Stephen Lytle.
      1. Esquivel, Laura, 1950—Miscellanea.   2. Authors, Mexican—
    20th century—Biography.   3. Cookery, Mexican.   I. Title:
    Between 2 fires.   II. Lytle, Stephen A.   III. Title.
    PQ7298.15.S638 Z46413 2001
    863'.64—dc21
    [B]   00-043134

ISBN 0-609-60847-9

10 9 8 7 6 5 4 3 2 1

First U.S. Edition

Contents

Prologue

$\mathcal{F}$irst of all, I want to thank Julio Ollero for his commitment in getting this anthology of texts published. For a long time I had ignored them because they seemed to have already fulfilled their intended duties and, like all finished work, achieved an independence that was beyond my control. Perhaps that is why, when Mercedes Casanovas, my literary agent, spoke to me about Julio's idea, my initial reaction was doubt. I saw myself obliged to confront work I hadn't looked at for some time and that, at least initially, appeared to have lost its original dynamism. A tentative study of these pieces, though, made me realize something I had not taken into account: the work continued to have significance outside the strict confines of the context in which it had been created. As I read the articles, speeches, and book prologues that make up this book, I recognized that there had been something very important I wanted to share in each of them. A sensation, a vital experience—maybe a gesture, or a smell, or a melody generated by each of the themes—that had been left out of the narration. Something had eluded me. I thought perhaps it was an "other voice." The "other voice," I concluded, is life itself, the experience of art brought to life. Any narration has profound significance when it is based closely on the intimacies of people's lives. For example, when a poem is rediscovered in the colors of the fruit in a market stall or when a novel is glimpsed in the intrepid face of a bank teller or in the taste of a meal prepared with passion and pleasure.

Additionally, republishing the texts seemed to create a conflict. I felt that putting them into circulation again could imply a

sterile act, primarily because of the inclusion
of a series of recipes that I wrote under very
particular circumstances: when *Like Water for
Chocolate* appeared, the editors at *Vogue* pro-
posed that I write a cooking column for the
magazine. They suggested I create, as I had in
the novel, a small story to accompany each
recipe. But the mechanism quickly wore
thin, and the experience, which at first had
seemed interesting, threatened to consume
itself and was becoming dangerously repetitive. I stopped writing the column before all
the possibilities were exhausted, and I considered the process definitively concluded.
Now all of a sudden I was to revive old recipes
whose time I firmly believed had already
passed. For me they represented work I had
left behind when I discovered that life was to
be lived somewhere else, and I was more
interested in going to the market to smell the
fruits and vegetables than in rereading old
work. But, I write. How was I supposed to deal

with the obvious contradiction: to live or to write? I thought about it a great deal, until I realized that there really was no contradiction. Life cannot be substituted for literature, nor can literature be substituted for life. Only those who try to deny one in favor of the other are trapped by a contradiction. No one who loves life can ignore literature, and no one who loves literature can ignore life. But to read is also to live: to live reading and to read life. To devote oneself exclusively to reading is to deny the vital motor principle of art: living life. The missing voice was life that comes and goes, to and from the literary work, because it is both its sustenance and its destination. It is imperative for us to remember that at certain points in our history we have forgotten one side or the other. By thinking too much about literature we forget to live, or by living we forget to turn literature into our experience. Having arrived at this conclusion, I breathed with relief. Seen from the proper perspective, the texts continued to be vital and were worthy of receiving a fresh look.

Having overcome that obstacle, I found myself with another. I had presented papers in several forums where I had spoken of an idea that obsesses me: the "New Man." This is an extremely important topic for me and it did not bother me to speak about it frequently on different occasions and in different countries to those in attendance, but I discovered that now, united in the same book, the pieces might seem repetitive. I was tempted to withhold some of them, but decided not to. I felt it was important, despite the risk, to emphasize the theme. Who is this New Man and why do I think it is so important to discuss the topic? The New Man is the individual that is able to integrate into his or her life the past and the lessons of the past, lost flavors, forgotten music, the faces of our grandparents, the memory of our dead. It is the person who never forgets that the most important thing is not production, but the individual who produces; that the well-being of people—all people—should be the principal objective in the development of human society. The New Man is a complete person who has been able to rise above the curse that haunts us and that has made us mutilated, unhappy beings. The New Man is someone who reads in life and who reads life, who reads literature and lives literature, and who lives life and rediscovers it in literature because the actions described there come from life. In this sense, republishing these texts has significance: to invoke life again through these small slices of intimacy, to remind people that it is imperative to read and to live with the same intensity; that without flavor life is not worth living; and that without the flavor of life, literature doesn't exist.

At the Hearth

I spent the first years of my life beside the hearth in my mother's and grandmother's kitchens, seeing how these wise women, upon entering those sacred places, became priestesses, great alchemists who dealt with water, air, fire, and earth—the four basic elements that comprise the entire universe. And the most surprising thing is that they did it in the most humble manner, as if they weren't doing anything, as if they weren't transforming the world with the purifying power of fire, as if they didn't know that the foods they prepared and the rest of us ate remained in our bodies for many hours, chemically altering our organisms, nourishing our souls and our spirits and giving us an identity, a language, a legacy.

It was there, at the hearth, where I received my first lessons about life from my mother. And where Saturnina, a servant newly arrived from the countryside, whom we affectionately called Sato, once prevented me from stepping on a kernel of corn that had fallen on the floor, because it sheltered the god of *maíz* inside, and he couldn't be disrespected in such a manner. The hearth, my family's favorite place for entertaining visitors, was where I learned what was going on in the world, and where my mother had long talks with my grandmother, my aunts, and from time to time some now deceased relative. Held there by the hypnotic power of the flames, I heard all kinds of stories, but mostly stories about women.

Then I had to leave home. I distanced myself completely from the kitchen. I had to study, to prepare myself for my future role in society. School was full of knowledge and surprises. For starters, I learned that two times two equals four, that dead people and rocks and plants can't talk, that there are no such things as ghosts, that the god of *maíz* and all the other gods belong to a magic, primitive realm and have no place in the rational, scientific, modern world. Oh, I learned so many things! At that time, I felt so superior to the poor women who spent their lives closed up in their kitchens. I felt sorry that no one had taken care of teaching them, among other things, that the god of *maíz* didn't exist. I believed that the truth about the universe was to be found in books and universities. With my diploma in one hand and the seed of revolution in the other, I was sure the world was going to open itself to me. The public world, of course, a world completely removed from the hearth.

During the sixties many of us participated in the continuing struggle started by other women at the beginning of the century. We felt that the urgent social changes needed at that point in time would take place outside the home and knew we had to join together, get out, fight. There was no time to waste, much less in the kitchen—a place that besides being disdained, along with household activities that we saw as simple acts with no transcendental significance—could only hinder our quest for greater knowledge, public awareness, and personal achievement. So, with the healthy intention of accomplishing important social changes that would culminate in the appearance of the New Man, we didn't think twice about giving up our intimate, private world in order to participate actively in society. Alongside our brothers, we took to the streets and handed out flowers and buttons. Our protest songs were heard everywhere. We wore pants and threw our bras out of windows.

While all this was happening and the New Man was being formed, an explosion of love caused me to marry an extraordinary man and give birth to a wonderful daughter. And I had to feed them. Not out of a sense of obligation, rather out of love. But the return to the kitchen was not easy. I wanted my daughter to know her past, to eat what I had eaten in my childhood; however, I quickly realized that I no longer remembered my family's recipes. At first I would call my mother on the telephone, but one day, frustrated with my poor memory, I forced myself to try and remember a recipe on my own. And that is how I discovered, as I had already known in my childhood, that it was possible to hear voices in the kitchen. I clearly heard my mother dictating the recipe step by step. Later, with a little more practice, I could hear

my dead grandmother's voice telling me how
to prepare one dish or another. I discovered
how gratifying it was to tell my daughter the
same stories I heard in front of the hearth
when I was a girl as I prepared our meals.
And that it was easier to cure her with my
mother's teas than with medicine. Little by
little, my return to the kitchen and my past
became so integrated that the day came when
I found myself preventing my daughter,
Sandra, from stepping on a kernel of corn
because it sheltered the god of *maíz*. I heard
myself saying that any respectable *salsa* had
to be made in a *molcajete*, not a blender, or
it wouldn't have any flavor. The time it took
to prepare didn't matter, because there is no
such thing as wasted time in the kitchen—
rather that is where we are able to recover
lost time.

And so, I was mortified to realize that my
daughter wasn't paying attention. Instead, she

was staring blankly at cartoons, forsaking the hypnotic power of fire for that of the television; the memory of the tribe, for commercials. I was so shocked I couldn't speak! Thousands of questions robbed me of my sleep. What had happened? Where had I gone wrong? What kind of society had we created? What had we women achieved by leaving the home? Yes, we had won rights that belonged to us and we had earned recognition for our intellectual activity and a better place in the world, but with great sadness I was forced to accept that none of the revolutions we participated in had managed to create a proper system for the creation of the New Man. He cannot come from a society out of balance, a society interested only in production and consumption, a society that doesn't equally satisfy the material and spiritual needs of human beings. An immediate change is necessary. We must adjust our value systems and

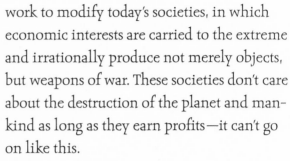

work to modify today's societies, in which economic interests are carried to the extreme and irrationally produce not merely objects, but weapons of war. These societies don't care about the destruction of the planet and mankind as long as they earn profits—it can't go on like this.

The arrival of a new revolution is imminent, and I don't think this time it will be from the outside in, but the opposite. It will entail the reclaiming of our rituals and ceremonies and the establishment of a new relationship with the land and the planet, with everything sacred. All this is possible in intimate spaces. It is there, around the hearth, where the New Man will appear, as the fruit of a common effort. He will give equal value to production and reproduction, to reason and emotion, to the intimate and the public, to the material and the spiritual. He will encourage the creation of balanced societies

and understand clearly that self-realization should not be linked solely to public recognition and economic retribution. He will question his active participation in society, asking himself whether he should work in a factory that grossly pollutes the environment even though he is well paid for his work, and will look for other ways to earn a living. He will value small acts for their intimacy and transcendence and understand that they modify society just as surely as public events do—each helping to elevate the human condition and allowing us to enter in communion with our past—and regard them as reminders of where we come from and where we should be headed.

So, suddenly I realized I needed to go back over the path we have taken to highlight the great advances we have achieved and to help restore the essential things we lost along the way. I wanted to share my doubts and my

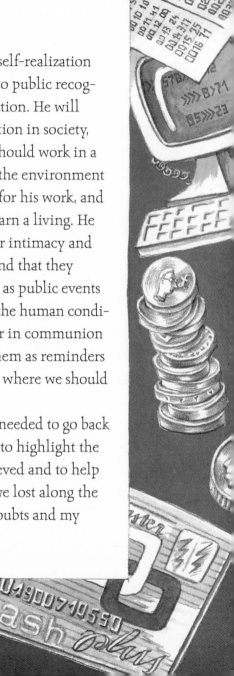

culinary, amorous, and cosmic experiences. So I wrote *Like Water for Chocolate*, which is merely the reflection of who I am as a woman, a wife, a mother, a daughter. Speaking of balanced beings, I must mention someone who is very important in my life and to whom I owe everything that I am: my father. From him I learned about laughter, tenderness, independence, generosity, and the joy of playing and creating. The love and respect I feel for him have allowed me to establish healthy relationships with the masculine world, and it is thanks to his wonderful influence that there is a balance between the masculine and feminine in my work. You'll have to forgive me this boldness, but I think women are very fortunate that men exist! The gods are very wise and certainly knew what they were doing. They created the sun and the moon, light and darkness, the eagle and the serpent, all for the same reason.

They are perfect complements and the mechanism we use to reach heaven.

In my life, this loving, passionate, intense
union of masculine and feminine has given
fruit to a book and a film that embrace my
family's past, my national conscience, my obsessions, my fears, my hopes, and more than
anything else, my belief in the love between
two people. A love that is now public and
circulates in theaters and bookstores all over
the world and which has made me worthy
of public acknowledgment. Acknowledgment that I feel compelled to share with my
mother, my daughter, my grandmother, my
sisters, with Sato and Tita, and all the women
before and after them who day by day, year
after year, have put us in contact with our true
origins. I also want to share it with all the
women who have not forgotten that stones do
speak and that the Earth is a living being.
And with those who transform each daily

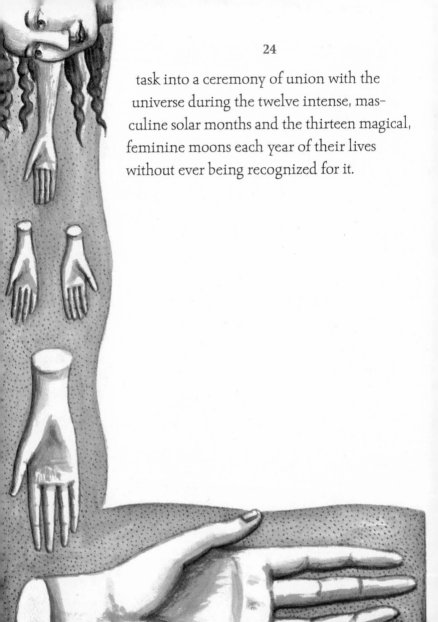

task into a ceremony of union with the
universe during the twelve intense, masculine solar months and the thirteen magical,
feminine moons each year of their lives
without ever being recognized for it.

God Is Above,
the Devil, Below!

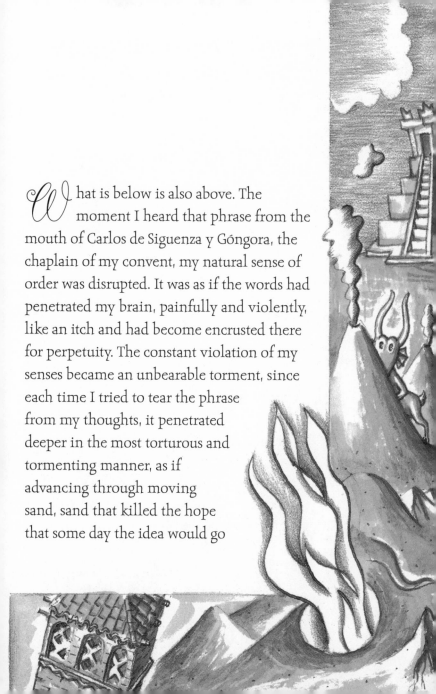

What is below is also above. The moment I heard that phrase from the mouth of Carlos de Siguenza y Góngora, the chaplain of my convent, my natural sense of order was disrupted. It was as if the words had penetrated my brain, painfully and violently, like an itch and had become encrusted there for perpetuity. The constant violation of my senses became an unbearable torment, since each time I tried to tear the phrase from my thoughts, it penetrated deeper in the most torturous and tormenting manner, as if advancing through moving sand, sand that killed the hope that some day the idea would go away and stop horrifying me and clouding my thoughts. The more don Carlos struggled to explain to me that "what is below is also above" refers to a universal law that establishes that the same conditions and phenomena that exist in this world occur, and are reproduced simultaneously, in another, higher plane, the less I understood.

If everything that exists on Earth has its equal in heaven, logically everything that is below Earth is the same as what is above, or on Earth and by extension in heaven, and that seemed to me to be terribly wrong, since it meant hell was the same as heaven and the Indians were the same as the Spaniards and that can't be, since the Indians, as their name indicates, are plebeian, ugly, sacrilegious, vile, sinful, dirty, dark-skinned heretics, and, as such, when they die they deserve to inhabit the kingdom of Satan,

exactly the opposite of us Spaniards of high rank who are white, Catholic, virtuous, and well mannered. What did I, the daughter of one of the best families in Nueva España, have in common with the pagan Indians who were buried below my house? What did my beautiful convent, La Concepción—which recently celebrated the opening of the first cathedral in the city built without adobe, and with round windows and a tower—have to do with the cruel, bloodthirsty architecture of the great pyramid Tenochtitlán? And what did my parents' ancestral manor have in common with the ruins of the temple below it and the savage, frenzied rituals the Indians held in it? Nothing. Absolutely nothing.

God made us Spaniards in his image and likeness, and the Indians were made in the horrendous image of Satan. But one terrible doubt began to seriously sicken me: what if the native Indians really wanted to be the

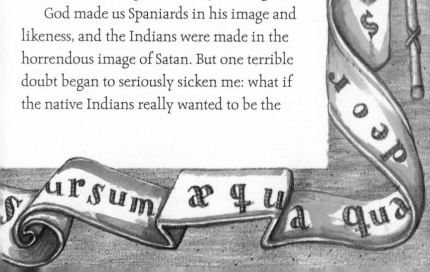

same as us and, using their intimate relationship with Lucifer, they tried, with his
malicious assistance, to make us lose the grace
of our birthright by presenting us, in a very
appealing manner, food grown in this Earth
that was poisoned with their blood? That
sinister Beelzebub already tried to tempt the
father of humanity with an apple in the
Garden of Eden, and he could well try to
repeat the incident. So I became obsessed
with the idea that all the food cultivated in
this malignant land was demonized and that
everyone who ate it entered into communion
with a world of horror and darkness, con-
demning his soul to hell. As a consequence,
I began to reject everything, from the most
beautiful flower to the most appetizing fruit,
that was of Mexican origin. The only foods
I would ingest had to be 100 percent Spanish
in origin, and under no circumstance would
I allow gastronomic *mestizaje.* This decision

was not at all easy to carry out if one has a capricious stomach like mine.

Aware of my weaknesses, when I reached the aqueduct that ran along the border of the palace and the main *plaza*, where Indian canoes slid past loaded with fruits, vegetables, grains and flowers, I forced myself not to look or smell or even imagine the presence of the *maíz*, beans, *chía*, tomato, squash, pineapple, chirimoya, papaya, capulines, avocado, mamey, *zapote*, *chicozapote*, *guayaba*, plums, *jocotes*, *tejocotes*, *pitahayas*, *chayote*, *chiles*, *anona*, and *chilacayote*. Usually I could avoid them without difficulty, as I did with the stands where frogs, ducks, guinea pigs, crayfish, and fly eggs were sold. But how could I avoid smelling *cacao*? How could I return to the cold and damp convent without drinking a cup of frothy hot chocolate? How could I abandon from one day to the next the delicious vice of drinking it? I had already

dominated my will and punished my stomach
for an entire month without touching the
forbidden food. A month without tasting
atole, *tamales*, *tortillas*, fruit conserves, and,
above all, without enjoying that marvelous
chocolate! So, without thinking further about
the consequences, I drank a large, delicious
cup in one long swallow and afterward, bur-
dened with regret, decided to return to my
cell. Trying to put my error out of my mind,
I walked along the merchants' arcade, lined
with stalls selling boots, shoes, dresses, shirts,
daggers, swords, silks, porcelain vases from
Castilla, and all the other things that I could
never buy or wear. But that didn't stop me
from dreaming about wearing a beautiful
shawl from Manila; once I had even imagined myself a handsome gentleman with a
cape and sword, but on this particular day my
imagination was disturbed by the foam from
the chocolate as it rose from my stomach to

my head, flooding my eyes and making them spin with thousands of iridescent, chocolate-colored circles. Inside of one of the tiny rings, I saw myself coming out of the belly of the city, in the center of the main *plaza*, along with an interminable throng of Indians dressed in rags and a procession of friars and monks. My hair was loose and my hips, covered by a skirt of coarse, transparent cloth, like those worn by the *mulatas*, were moving in a lascivious manner. Before me was the main temple of Tenochtitlán, and along its high, narrow steps, Spanish nuns and priests ascended to the thirteen celestial strata. I tried to climb with them, but the Indians hindered me. They tore off my clothes and left me nude and stunned in the face of their incessant shouting of proclamations, the deafening ringing of the bells, and the scandalous noise from the wheels of the viceroy's carriage as it made its way to the palace. I ran through a dark tunnel, descending little by little to Mictiana, the deepest of the underworlds. But God, blessed may He be, always benign and merciful, didn't abandon me in the midst of the chaos reigning in my mind and illuminated my consciousness with a ray of light so I could control my destiny and find my way. I ran to the entrance of the cathedral, where I threw myself on the floor and licked the tiles. I licked them as I moved toward the main altar until my tongue was dry and sore and no trace of saliva or that damned chocolate remained. I begged forgiveness a thousand times as I pulled down and destroyed the statues of saints that adorned the nave of the temple. The Supreme Creator heard me and gave me His absolution because He knows the truth and He knows that, really, the Indians and the Spaniards are the same. He knows the priests from the Holy See are the same Aztec priests sacrificing human lives

to honor him, and that, really, each of the Aztec idols is the same as one of the statues of the saints. He knows that, really, Lucifer was made in his image and likeness. He knows that, just as the Aztec priests drank blood and ate the bodies of those they sacrificed, so the Spanish priests drank Christ's blood and ate His body, and finally that, when one drinks chocolate she enters into communion with Mictián, but by the same token, at the same time, with the highest spheres of heaven, since "what is below is also above."

Now, all I have to do is explain this to the inquisitors from the Holy See who are coming to judge me tomorrow.

Apple Soup

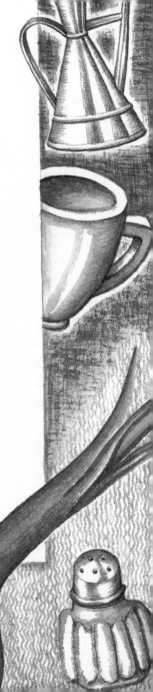

Ingredients

3 apples
6 cups of chicken broth
2 *jitomates*
1 onion
2 tablespoons of flour
1 tablespoon of parsley
oil
salt
pepper

$\mathcal{P}$eel the apples, then cut them into quarters and soak in enough water to cover, with a tablespoon of salt so they stay white. Ever since I can remember, this soup was prepared in our house each time my uncle came to visit us in the capital. While I helped my mother, I listened to her tell how intelligent, handsome, and kind my uncle was. My mother's words were like a proud gas inside me, inflating my chest as if it were a balloon and hardening it with pride. I felt so important being a member of the Romero family! In all of Mexico there couldn't be a better ancestral lineage. Inevitably, as the flour assumed a golden hue in the oil, there would be talk of my portentous uncle's new

business interests. And while my mother chopped the *jitomates* and onion and put them on the stove to simmer until they softened, she would recount my uncle's most recent acquisitions.

It was one of those afternoons, while I was dutifully stirring the broth so it wouldn't clump, when I heard that my uncle had been called by the governor to assume a political post in the state of Tabasco. I had no idea what kind of work a politician did, but judging by my mother's boastful reaction, I imagined that it must be very important and well paid. Shortly thereafter, this was corroborated when I saw the increase in the cost of the gifts he brought on his visits and the changes in his lifestyle. He began to travel to the capital and abroad more frequently. He could afford the luxury of trips to Europe, China, Japan, and other exotic places. Our house was filled with strange objects that we could brag about to our neighbors.

When my uncle announced an impending visit to our house, we would immediately begin to prepare apple soup—his favorite dish, even though he had eaten in the best restaurants in the world. We took such great care with its preparation! In our desire to please him we became experts. We knew exactly what size to cut the pieces of fruit, at what instant to stop browning the flour and to add the *jitomates*, the precise moment when it had cooked enough to add the broth and the salt and pepper, and the perfect time to add the well-drained apples and the parsley. We let it boil until it was cooked just the way my uncle liked it and then removed it from the stove. I don't remember a single time that it came out badly in all those years.

But since my uncle was assassinated last year it hasn't turned out right. I don't know

why. I don't know whether my uncle's ghost impregnates the soup with an unpleasant flavor or whether it's because when we went to his funeral in Tabasco we learned that everyone hated him. Or maybe it's because we found out that he had robbed and killed many men. Or because we discovered that he had been lying to us, and his real job was drug trafficking, not politics. Or because he left a lot of children penniless, and we felt responsible for them. Or maybe it was because he took from us the feeling of pride we had in having a prominent relative. I don't know. But the reality is that our apple soup doesn't taste the same anymore.

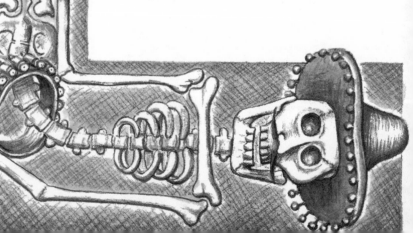

Between Two Fires

The people in small towns use sayings that express great wisdom. I frequently make use of them because they reveal universal truths. "Like water for chocolate" is one that is very well known to many of you. One of my favorites is: "Love is repaid with love." Nothing could be truer. The only value comparable to love is love itself. Neither gold, nor *quetzal* feathers, nor precious stones can equal it. It has worth greater than all else. And I have found that anything worthwhile is realized by and through love.

From its conception, my novel, *Like Water for Chocolate*, was surrounded by love. Its gestation began not when the story's central idea occurred to me, but when I took my first bite of food prepared with love.

I wrote the book in an attempt to give proper importance to the transmission of love in the kitchen. I am convinced that we can imprint this emotion on others through food, as Tita does in the novel, and through all of our daily activities. When this affectionate power is strong enough, it is impossible not to perceive it. Others can sense it, feel it, enjoy it. This is proven to me more and more each day. I wrote my novel with love, and my agents, my editors, my translators, and my distributors felt it. They returned that love to me and spread it to others. And I am more than satisfied with the "compensation" my work has generated. Now, this book is the final link in a loving chain.

So, I have no option but to thank everyone dead or alive, present or absent, who contributed air, earth, fire, and water to *Appetite for Passion*. This book's existence reconfirms my belief that in matters of love and cooking there are no borders. Everything I have eaten, the people I have eaten with, and the manner in which I have eaten have determined what I am. And I have to admit here that a certain amount of Coca-Cola runs through my veins.

I'll explain. Many of you know that my mother's family is from the city of Piedras Negras in the Mexican state of Coahuila. When I was a young girl I thought Piedras Negras started in Coahuila and ended in San Antonio, Texas. Its city limits were endless, or at least they seemed so to me. Perhaps because when I was a little girl geography was puzzling to me. All that talk about from this tree to over there is another place wasn't

clear in my head. I only knew what I liked.
I had to spend several years in school before
I could accept that borders and hate existed
between towns.

Every year my family traveled from
Mexico City to San Antonio, Texas, to visit
our relatives who lived there. Along the way
we stopped to see friends in Piedras Negras.
In each city the magic was repeated: the
alchemy in the kitchen, the ceremonies, the
powerful transmission of love through food.
The only difference was that in Piedras
Negras I devoured wheat tortillas, *machaca*
with eggs, and *dulce de leche con nuez,* and in
San Antonio I was crazy about glazed doughnuts and Milky Way bars. And since *How to
Read Donald Duck* hadn't been written yet,
I wasn't embarrassed to read Walt Disney
magazines during the trips.

The years passed and my knowledge

of geography increased. My advances were notable. In no time at all I understood that Piedras Negras didn't extend to San Antonio. I learned that one city was in the United States and the other was in Mexico. And that there were borders between them, and something more: that American culture had very little to do with Mexican culture, even though my sisters and I organized gatherings every Saturday where we served sandwiches and Coca-Cola, danced rock and roll, and chewed gum. We had a justification for everything: the sandwiches were a variation on our own *tortas,* and the *tortas*—we didn't go so far as to discuss their origin—they were Mexican, period. Our enjoyment of chewing gum came from the Aztecs—before the Spanish arrived they had chewed *chapopote.* There was nothing wrong with rock and roll—besides, it was an international phenomenon—and Coca-Cola had been invented for medicinal purposes, so drinking it had to be good for us, didn't it?

More years went by and my knowledge about geography continued to increase. I learned where Vietnam was. I learned that it was divided in two. I learned that my cousin from San Antonio had been called to serve in the army. That's when Coca-Cola began tasting bitter. I learned it was bad for my teeth and my health. We started calling it "the black water of Yankee imperialism." I stopped drinking it. I was afraid it would bring the horror of the war to me. Fortunately hippies appeared on my geographic map. I learned where U.C. Berkeley was and what happened there. In Mexico, young people took to the streets and we handed out flowers and listened to Joan Baez and laughed and made love freely and believed

that the birth of a New Man was possible—
we thought we could change the world. But
we couldn't, and for a long time I kept
asking myself what went wrong.

Why weren't any of our revolutions able
to create the right system for the New Man
to appear? Where had all the hippies gone?
Was Joan Baez still singing? What had
happened to all the people from Woodstock?

The success of my novel gave me the
answers. It allowed me to travel around
the United States, and I realized I wasn't
the only person who was worried about
establishing a new relationship with the
Earth, the universe, with everything sacred.
Many other people had discovered that the
new revolution was going to originate in
the intimate world of rituals and ceremonies. Like me, they were desperately
trying to substitute spiritual values for

material ones, and they were preserving the power of fire in their homes. This book is the palpable proof.

Not only that, but it also proves that I was right as a child. Borders don't exist! It's a lie that a dividing line separates one town from another. It's a lie that the hippies sang in vain: they planted a seed. It's a lie that Americans don't eat *chile* and beans—they love our food. It's a lie that Mexicans don't eat hamburgers—we love to make them, we just add more spices.

Now I know that hope isn't dead—the New Man is coming. And he's going to be completely ignorant about geography; he won't care whether the ground he walks on is on this side or the other; he will eat *tortillas* with the same pleasure that he drinks Coca-Cola. He will know the important thing is not what he is eating, but that he is participating in a ceremony that returns him to his origin—to his cosmic origin, which goes far beyond ethnicity. So if that's where we're going and we Mexicans are the children of corn, then Americans have already eaten enough popcorn to be our cousins.

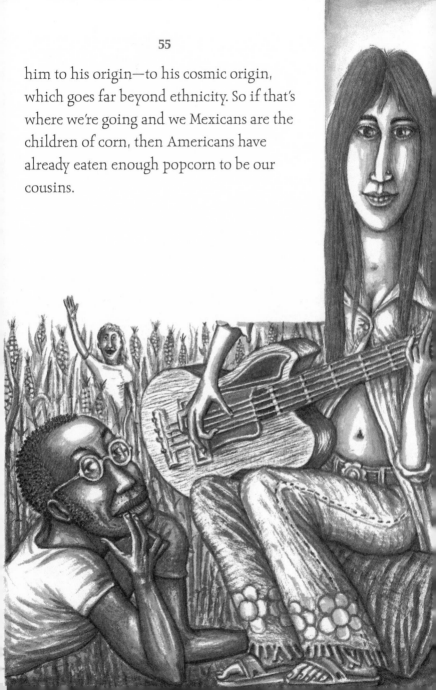

Oaxacan Black Mole

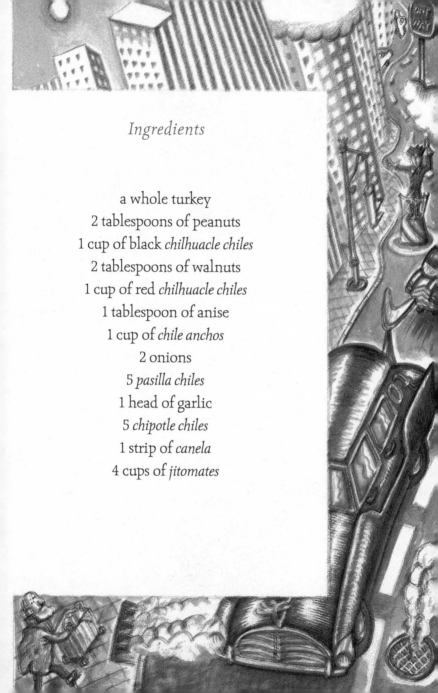

Ingredients

a whole turkey
2 tablespoons of peanuts
1 cup of black *chilhuacle chiles*
2 tablespoons of walnuts
1 cup of red *chilhuacle chiles*
1 tablespoon of anise
1 cup of *chile anchos*
2 onions
5 *pasilla chiles*
1 head of garlic
5 *chipotle chiles*
1 strip of *canela*
4 cups of *jitomates*

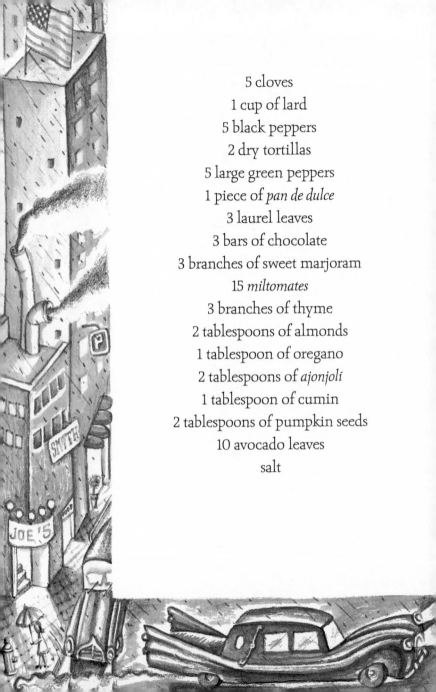

5 cloves
1 cup of lard
5 black peppers
2 dry tortillas
5 large green peppers
1 piece of *pan de dulce*
3 laurel leaves
3 bars of chocolate
3 branches of sweet marjoram
15 *miltomates*
3 branches of thyme
2 tablespoons of almonds
1 tablespoon of oregano
2 tablespoons of *ajonjolí*
1 tablespoon of cumin
2 tablespoons of pumpkin seeds
10 avocado leaves
salt

C lean the turkey, cut it in pieces, and put it on the fire to cook in enough water to cover, along with a piece of onion and two cloves of garlic. As I read my pious mother's recipe I can't help feeling thankful that I spent a large portion of my childhood watching her cook while I did my homework at the kitchen table. If not for those experiences, I never would have known that you have to skim off the foam that forms on broth as it starts to boil. I don't know why that kind of information is left out of recipes—it's as if the cooks think everyone should already know these details beforehand. Where does it say that after peeling and deveining *chiles* you have to wash your fingers with a piece of lemon? It cost me a whole afternoon with a sore, red eye to learn that bit of kitchen wisdom when I was a little girl—after making the mistake of trying to remove a speck of dust with fingers that had handled *chiles.* Luckily, it never happened to me again.

Now that I live in New York, far from home and my mother's kitchen, the need to prepare decent food has led me to make all sorts of foolish mistakes. The group of students I share an apartment with on 25th Street near the East River has had to suffer the consequences of my culinary apprenticeship along with me. They're used to saving time and so fulfill their commitment to prepare dinner once a week by opening a can of soup, mixing it with hot water from the tap and giving it to the rest of us to eat—from the can so they don't have to wash any dishes! They can't understand how I can spend an entire afternoon cooking a Oaxacan *mole*—wasting time and risking all kinds of accidents.

But what can you expect from people who have eaten frozen or canned food, sitting on the floor watching television, since they were born? They've never experienced it, so they can't know how wonderful it is to come home to the smell of freshly cooked beans, a rich stew, or a delicious *mole* and to eat it on a clean tablecloth with hot *tortillas* along with the rest of their family. Mmmm, hot *tortillas!* In the middle of the winter, so dark and cold, how nice it would be to feel a little warmth: the heat of my mother's kitchen, the heat from the plants in our house at midday, the heat that stays in my throat and stomach after eating *mole.* I can't go on. I even miss the heat from the *metro!* Seriously, the fact is that in this city, where it now gets dark at four in the afternoon, the sun can't warm you. The hope of relieving a little of the numbness in my soul drove me to gather the last of my transportation money for the week and head for the corner of 14th Street and Seventh Avenue, where my little oasis can be found: La Casa Moneo, a small store that sells Mexican products. There I found all the ingredients I was looking for, from dried *chiles* to sweet, delicious *conchas*.

Jimmy, one of my roommates, coughs when he breathes the fumes from the *chiles* I am frying in the lard. He has come into the kitchen several times for a glass of water and each time looks at me reproachfully for contaminating his air, but I don't care. His canned soups bother me more than a little cooking smell could ever bother him, but I never say anything. Besides, I only have two *chiles* left to fry. Then I just have to fry the garlic, onion, *tortillas,* and the *conchas* in the same skillet. Everything else is ready. I prepare it exactly as the recipe dictates, well, except that I did have to substitute the skillet for a *comal* to toast the almonds, *ajonjolí*, peanuts, walnuts, and pumpkin seeds. Then, instead of grinding them in a *metate*, the way I should have, I had to use a food processor. And since I don't have a *molcajete* either, I used the same machine to grind the peppers, cloves, anise, cumin, oregano, *canela*, and the laurel leaves, sweet marjoram, and thyme. I just hope it doesn't alter the taste of the food. Mixing these ingredients with the turkey broth, I make the *mole* sauce. Separately, I chop the *jitomates* and *miltomates* in the blender and put the resulting mixture on the stove to simmer with a little lard and later add the *mole* sauce. Finally, I toast the avocado leaves and add them to the *mole* along with the salt. It's important to prepare the *mole* a day before, so the flavor has a chance to develop.

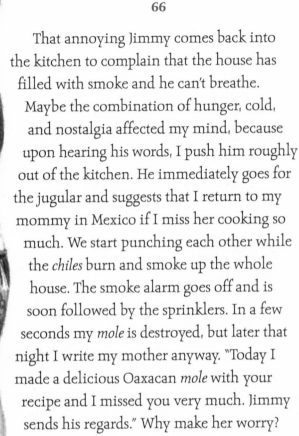

That annoying Jimmy comes back into the kitchen to complain that the house has filled with smoke and he can't breathe. Maybe the combination of hunger, cold, and nostalgia affected my mind, because upon hearing his words, I push him roughly out of the kitchen. He immediately goes for the jugular and suggests that I return to my mommy in Mexico if I miss her cooking so much. We start punching each other while the *chiles* burn and smoke up the whole house. The smoke alarm goes off and is soon followed by the sprinklers. In a few seconds my *mole* is destroyed, but later that night I write my mother anyway. "Today I made a delicious Oaxacan *mole* with your recipe and I missed you very much. Jimmy sends his regards." Why make her worry?

Intimate Succulencies

*A Philosophic Treatise
on Cooking*

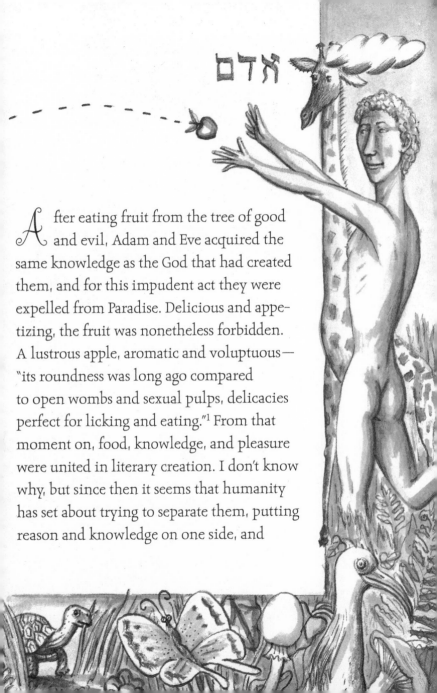

אדם

After eating fruit from the tree of good and evil, Adam and Eve acquired the same knowledge as the God that had created them, and for this impudent act they were expelled from Paradise. Delicious and appetizing, the fruit was nonetheless forbidden. A lustrous apple, aromatic and voluptuous— "its roundness was long ago compared to open wombs and sexual pulps, delicacies perfect for licking and eating."[1] From that moment on, food, knowledge, and pleasure were united in literary creation. I don't know why, but since then it seems that humanity has set about trying to separate them, putting reason and knowledge on one side, and

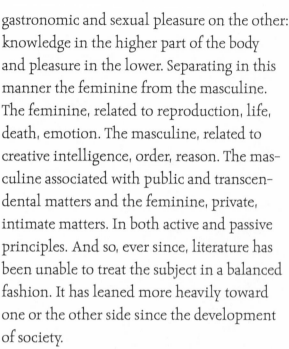

gastronomic and sexual pleasure on the other: knowledge in the higher part of the body and pleasure in the lower. Separating in this manner the feminine from the masculine. The feminine, related to reproduction, life, death, emotion. The masculine, related to creative intelligence, order, reason. The masculine associated with public and transcendental matters and the feminine, private, intimate matters. In both active and passive principles. And so, ever since, literature has been unable to treat the subject in a balanced fashion. It has leaned more heavily toward one or the other side since the development of society.

As human society developed, man came to know nature and its laws to the extent that he was capable of transforming them. It is said that the great civilizations were born at the moment when woman first discovered how to cultivate plants. The tribe then became sedentary and began to modify its immediate environment. Gathering around the fire and eating in a planned, rather than random, fashion is how man became man. Around the fire with the tribe, he learned the principles of science that were later transferred to books and universities. When they tried to intellectually castrate Sor Juana, she was prohibited from having any contact with books, as if they were the only source of knowledge. Perhaps they had already forgotten the original source of knowledge. Sor Juana took refuge in the kitchen and, of course, continued learning.

> . . . I see that an egg congeals and fries in lard or oil and, on the contrary, it disintegrates in syrup; I see that for sugar to remain liquid it is enough to add a minimal amount of water in which *membrillo* or another bitter fruit has soaked. . . . And I must say upon seeing these things: if

Aristotle had cooked, he would have written much more.[2]

Nevertheless, progress obliged women to abandon this refuge of creation and knowledge. One of the important changes in this century has been the incorporation of women into the workforce. Women have given up working in the home, which Lenin referred to in this manner:

> In the majority of cases, domestic labor is the most unproductive, the most barbaric and the most arduous activity for a woman. It is exceptionally wretched and is bereft of anything whatsoever which could promote the development of women.[3]

It was thought that real change and development, not only for women, but also for society, would be generated outside the home.

It seemed that reproduction (feminine) was not as important as production (masculine). Progress snatched the creative and generating fire of life from women by removing them from the home and using them in factories. Women, effectively, abandoned their homes and were given an opportunity to develop themselves and to participate enthusiastically in the revolutionary movements of this century, which will culminate in the arrival of the New Man.

At that early stage society was inclined toward public endeavors, production, the masculine. What options for integration did women have within that type of society? Very few. What was life like for a thinking woman? It must have been insufferable, according to the literature of women writers of the era.

I will ruminate, in silence, on my rancor. I am always assigned the responsibilities

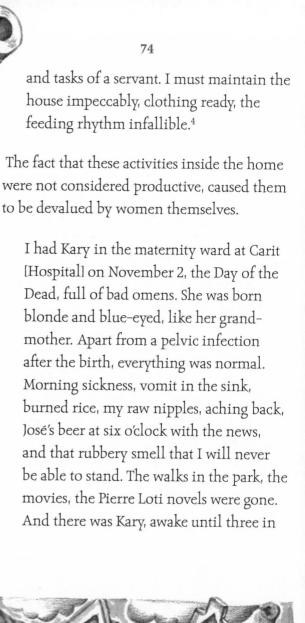

and tasks of a servant. I must maintain the house impeccably, clothing ready, the feeding rhythm infallible.[4]

The fact that these activities inside the home were not considered productive, caused them to be devalued by women themselves.

I had Kary in the maternity ward at Carit [Hospital] on November 2, the Day of the Dead, full of bad omens. She was born blonde and blue-eyed, like her grand-mother. Apart from a pelvic infection after the birth, everything was normal. Morning sickness, vomit in the sink, burned rice, my raw nipples, aching back, José's beer at six o'clock with the news, and that rubbery smell that I will never be able to stand. The walks in the park, the movies, the Pierre Loti novels were gone. And there was Kary, awake until three in the morning while José snored and farted mercilessly.[5]

It seemed that any life worth living was still found outside the home. Maternity, the giving of life, wasn't seen as a productive activity in itself, but rather as a bothersome activity that removed women from mass production and public performance. Inside the home there was only death, represented by routine and depression. And what really existed outside the home? Death and repression. The external fire was converted into weapons for the war that was destroying life. Religion legislated pleasure and controlled the sexual relations of couples. Women felt like simple objects for reproduction and support of the production of men. We were no longer considered the generating center of life and society. Seen in this manner, it's logical that literature written by women

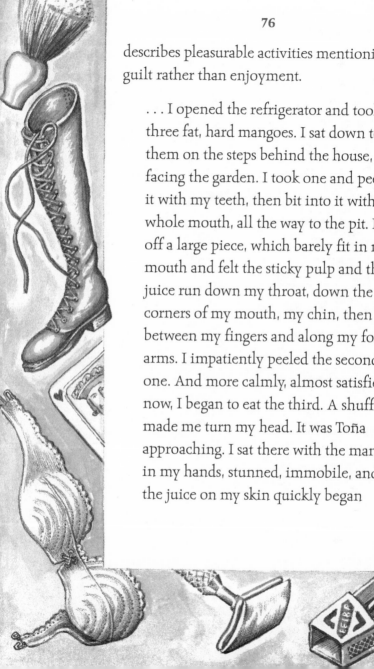

describes pleasurable activities mentioning guilt rather than enjoyment.

> . . . I opened the refrigerator and took out three fat, hard mangoes. I sat down to eat them on the steps behind the house, facing the garden. I took one and peeled it with my teeth, then bit into it with my whole mouth, all the way to the pit. I tore off a large piece, which barely fit in my mouth and felt the sticky pulp and the juice run down my throat, down the corners of my mouth, my chin, then between my fingers and along my fore-arms. I impatiently peeled the second one. And more calmly, almost satisfied now, I began to eat the third. A shuffling made me turn my head. It was Toña approaching. I sat there with the mango in my hands, stunned, immobile, and the juice on my skin quickly began

to dry, making me feel uncomfortable and dirty.[6]

Fortunately, it seems things are changing. Contraception has liberated women from the dangers of pregnancy and has disassociated the sexual experience from reproduction. Little by little, the moral and religious preconceptions that contaminated a couple's relationship have begun to disappear. Women have begun to feel like subjects instead of objects. All these changes in society have brought enormous benefits to women, but at the same time, they have filled us with contradictions. It is true that we can now study and work without restrictions and participate actively in society, but this participation is determined by our intimate relationship with our children, our sexuality, fire, alchemy, the home, life. As with masculine and feminine, the rational

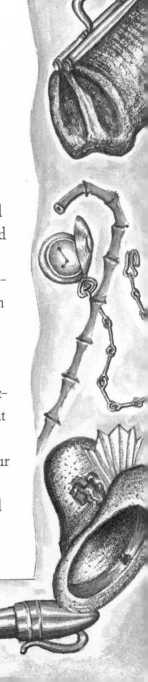

and emotional are not clearly delineated, as if this splitting of the body in half is not as noticeable in reality. And so we find women who, while using their creative intelligence to write—normally classified as masculine— still choose to have children. We feel another life inside our bodies, enjoy the pleasures of sex—well, I wish this were the case for the majority. We live day to day with life and death and have direct contact with the elements that form the world and its laws. We know how to transform and purify these elements with fire. All of these are classified as feminine.

Tita, kneeling and bent over the grinding stone, moved with a steady rhythm as she ground the almonds and *ajonjolí*. Beneath her blouse her breasts swayed freely since she never wore a brassiere. . . . They remained in amorous ecstasy until Pedro lowered his gaze and locked it on Tita's

breasts. She stopped grinding, straight-
ened up, and proudly thrust out her chest,
so that Pedro could enjoy it fully. His gaze
on her breasts changed forever the relationship between them. After the intense
stare that penetrated her clothing, nothing would ever be the same. Tita felt for
herself how contact with fire alters the
elements, how a ball of dough becomes
tortilla, how a breast never touched by the
flame of love is an inert breast, a useless
ball of dough.[7]

And now surprisingly, we are approach-
ing the end of the century and the New Man
still has not appeared. No revolution has
created him. Because no government is eager
for him to surface. Because he would have
to be a man with humane values, and a man
with those characteristics would not fit into
the system, into any of the systems that exist
today. Because he would be a man who

defended life before anything else and would surely disobey the order to activate the bomb that would destroy the planet. And where is the school that can shape a being who questions, is argumentative, is disobedient, when all education is oriented toward obedience and integration into the system? The appearance of this man must be the result of the individual labor and conscious effort of a couple, but today couples are busy irrationally producing and consuming. This new being has to know where he is coming from and where he is going. He has to be in alimentary communion with his past, connecting him to his origin, and that is no longer possible. We have lost our rituals, our ceremonies. Modernity has cut us off from them. Man is lost in a labyrinth of identical products. Our houses, clothing, canned food. Human beings are desperately searching for a way out. Looking for the countryside not the metropolis, artisans not bureaucrats, direct democracy not bureaucracy.[8]

There is a thread that can take us there and it is nothing more or less than nostalgia for the past. Nostalgia has to do with that which we have lost, with rituals, the intimate, the emotional, the feminine. We must re-establish a more individualized and humane relationship with nature. We need contemporary Prometheuses to steal the fire from industry and the weapons factories that pollute and produce irrationally to give it back to man in order to save him. To rescue the creative power of fire and bring it to the home. To reestablish the kitchen as a place for learning, where art and life are created. Where the products of the earth are combined with those of the air, the present with the past. Where active and passive principles mix, they form another artistic and spiritual reality through an act of love. Only love can

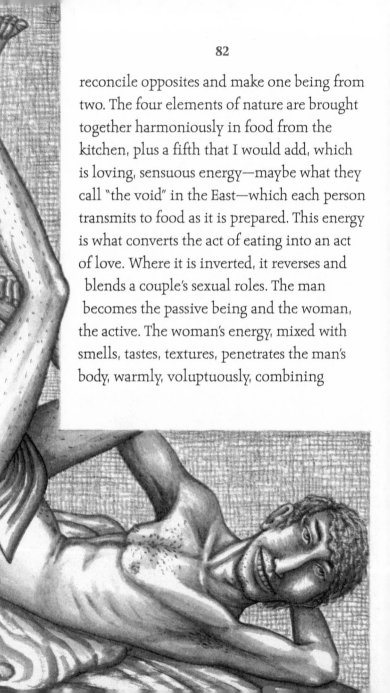

reconcile opposites and make one being from two. The four elements of nature are brought together harmoniously in food from the kitchen, plus a fifth that I would add, which is loving, sensuous energy—maybe what they call "the void" in the East—which each person transmits to food as it is prepared. This energy is what converts the act of eating into an act of love. Where it is inverted, it reverses and blends a couple's sexual roles. The man becomes the passive being and the woman, the active. The woman's energy, mixed with smells, tastes, textures, penetrates the man's body, warmly, voluptuously, combining

sexual and gastronomic pleasure. There is
no battle of the sexes here. The usual rules are
vanquished. There is only one great pleasure.
We must nurture and rescue our rituals. By
this means we regain our spirit. So then we
have in our hands, women and men both,
the opportunity to return to the homes that
we abandoned, but consciously now and at
another level. And together we sanctify our
homes, making them once again a place for
communion with the universe. We rediscover
the fire and the sacred food that will take us
back to our past, the source of our future. To
a familiar, common past, to our precious
homeland. Then we must go further, mixing
pleasure and knowledge, to look for the secret
formula of the forbidden fruit which, when
we eat it, will return us to Eden.

We will once again transform ourselves
into gods. Become naked like Adam and Eve.
Maybe once the principles of active and

passive, rational and emotional, masculine and feminine are joined together again in a pleasurable, lustful, orgiastic manner, the new civilization will appear, along with the New Man, and a new literature that speaks, without regret or shame, of the home, of love, of the kitchen, of life.

Notes

1. María Luisa Mendoza, "Fruta madura de ida," in *Ojos de papel volando* (Mexico: Joaquín Mortiz, 1985).
2. Sor Juana Inés de la Cruz, *Respuesta a Sor Filotea de la Cruz* (Barcelona: Editorial Laertes, 1979).
3. V. I. Lenin, *Complete Works*, vol. 30 (Moscow: Foreign Language Edition, 1950).
4. Rosario Castallenos, "Lección de cocina," in *Album de familia* (Mexico: Joaquín Mortiz, 1990).
5. Dorelia Barahona, *De qué manera te olvido* (Mexico: Editorial Era, 1990).
6. "La señal," in *Obras completas de Ines Arredondo* (Mexico: Siglo XXI Editores, 1988).
7. Laura Esquivel, *Como agua para chocolate* (Mexico: Editorial Planeta, 1989).
8. Octavio Paz, "La mesa y el lecho" in *El ogro filantrópico* (Mexico: Joaquín Mortiz, 1991).

Manchamanteles

Ingredients

2 pounds of pork shoulder, sliced
2 plantains
3 slices of pineapple
1/2 onion
1/2 head of garlic
1/4 strip of *canela*
6 black peppers
4 cloves
1/4 cup of sugar
jitomates
cumin
ground oregano
chile anchos for seasoning
lard
salt

*O*h, miserable me! Oh, poor, unhappy
me—! If you knew what I have suffered
in this cruel world! My worst sin was being
born. My mere presence is a bother and as
soon as I get settled somewhere I am immediately removed by force. It would have been
better if I had been born a lizard, an ant, or
even a rat, but not a cockroach! And if they
were going to make me an insect, why
couldn't they have given me some wings with
nice colors like the dragonflies or an internal
glow like the fireflies? I mean, anything to
make my appearance less repulsive, since
because of it I have to spend my life like an
ugly doll, hidden in dark corners and eating
only waste. Yes, don't be afraid, garbage. They

tell me it's the cockroach's mission in this life.
Malarkey! We haven't been given any other,
since we barely set foot in the light and—
POW!—we get swept away or kicked or
crushed. Who told everybody we don't like
fine food? Good wine? A nicely set table?

If we were given an opportunity to perform in society, we could prove ourselves.
Like that time I dared to come out of my
hiding place to visit doña Asunción de la
Riva. It was like a dream. I had spent a terrible
night in doña Paquita's house, freezing to
death and my legs aching. My spirits were
very low. A cockroach smashed by a bus on
the highway couldn't have felt worse than I
did. And I asked myself, Why do cockroaches
have to suffer? Why do I have to live in this
miserable house that doesn't even have any
waste? Just because they don't have enough
money for insecticides? No! Enough! I have
the right, like any other inhabitant of this

planet, to better living conditions. And
having said that, I packed my things and left
doña Paquita's pigpen for good. I headed
straight for an elegant house in Lomas de
Chapultepec and settled myself immediately
in a corner of the modern kitchen. Such
comfort! Such pleasing warmth! Such aromas!
Someone was frying plantains. It didn't take
me long to figure out from the smell that
they were preparing some delicious *manchamanteles*. Yummm! What a good start for this
new phase of my life!

Cautiously I stuck my head out a bit to
enjoy the spectacle and watched Juanita, the
cook, frying the meat in a casserole with a
little oil and later adding water and some salt.
Separately, she started to peel the *chile anchos;*
first she toasted them over the stove, being
careful not to burn them (because they can
turn bitter), then set them aside for the skins
to soften. Next she chopped them with the

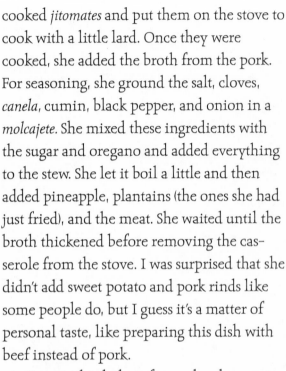

cooked *jitomates* and put them on the stove to cook with a little lard. Once they were cooked, she added the broth from the pork. For seasoning, she ground the salt, cloves, *canela*, cumin, black pepper, and onion in a *molcajete*. She mixed these ingredients with the sugar and oregano and added everything to the stew. She let it boil a little and then added pineapple, plantains (the ones she had just fried), and the meat. She waited until the broth thickened before removing the casserole from the stove. I was surprised that she didn't add sweet potato and pork rinds like some people do, but I guess it's a matter of personal taste, like preparing this dish with beef instead of pork.

Do you think that after such a demonstration of this country's culinary art I wasn't going to be tempted to take a little taste before everybody else? Summoning up all my courage, I quickly scurried across the kitchen

toward the table where Juanita had placed the
delicious dish. I climbed up one of the table
legs and, now feeling confident, I dived right
into the *manchamanteles*. Mmmm! I was in
heaven with my first mouthful. My spirits
soared and for an instant I felt as if I were
floating in the clouds. Well, I was literally
traveling through space since, to my great
dismay, I realized I was being carried to the
dining room table. Lying face up I was able to
enjoy the marvelous spectacle of the light
reflected in the crystal lamps during the trip.
And once I reached the table my soul entered
ecstasy. I had never seen such a beautifully
decorated table. The gleaming silver dazzled
me so that my confused mind was filled with
a series of images of glowing, transparent
cockroaches, accompanied by heavenly crys-
talline sounds. A brilliant ray of light invited
me to move farther out into this wonderful
world of light, but as I moved I was discovered

by one of the dinner guests, who, terrified, threw me from the table and bounced me off the wall. Then my dream ended and here I am again, in poverty, longing for the luxurious state in which I once found myself. Like Calderón de la Barca would say, "Life is a dream and dreams are just dreams."

Introduction to Bread

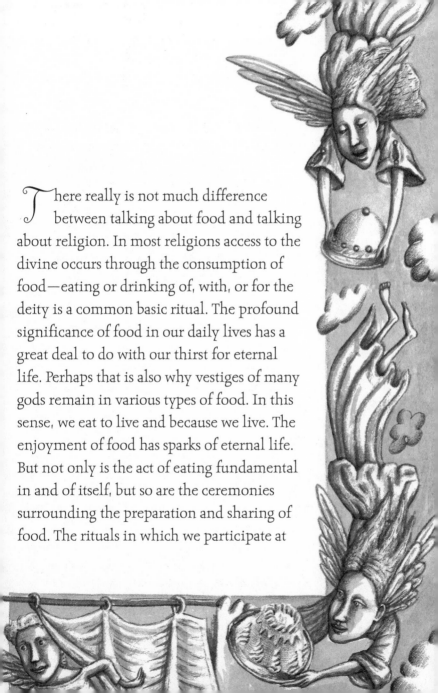

There really is not much difference between talking about food and talking about religion. In most religions access to the divine occurs through the consumption of food—eating or drinking of, with, or for the deity is a common basic ritual. The profound significance of food in our daily lives has a great deal to do with our thirst for eternal life. Perhaps that is also why vestiges of many gods remain in various types of food. In this sense, we eat to live and because we live. The enjoyment of food has sparks of eternal life. But not only is the act of eating fundamental in and of itself, but so are the ceremonies surrounding the preparation and sharing of food. The rituals in which we participate at the table are rich with ancient religious significance. It is not a coincidence, then, that some religions utilize the evening meal or a fraternal gathering around a table to symbolize deeper spiritual mysteries. So, of course, discussing the preparation of bread would have special meaning for us. In Christian cultures, the presence of bread implies the memory of the passionate life, death, and resurrection of the Son of God, whose body "through simple accidents, makes use of grains of wheat, to convert them into his flesh," as the famous Mexican baroque poetess Sor Juana Inés de la Cruz wrote.

The breaking of bread is an excellent symbol for the resurrection of the Messiah. Through the ritual of Communion, the departed Master returned to physically and spiritually nourish his disciples in the form of bread and wine. This is why religious communities have always valued the importance of nourishment and consider it a sacrament—the literal presence of God among men—and have developed subtle, marvelous ways to symbolize the different forms of performing the loving act of preparing food for the enjoyment of their brothers.

In this book you will find recipes for preparing bread from different Jesuit communities, assembled by my dear friend Rick Curry.

Though we may not all be religious, I don't think it would be hard for any of us to acknowledge that through the smells and tastes of food we share with others, and the sustaining presence of the divine inherent in them, we can enjoy a glimpse of paradise every day.

Chestnut Soufflé

Ingredients

25 chestnuts
2 ounces of butter
4 cups of milk
2 tablespoons of flour
7 eggs
1/2 cup of powdered sugar

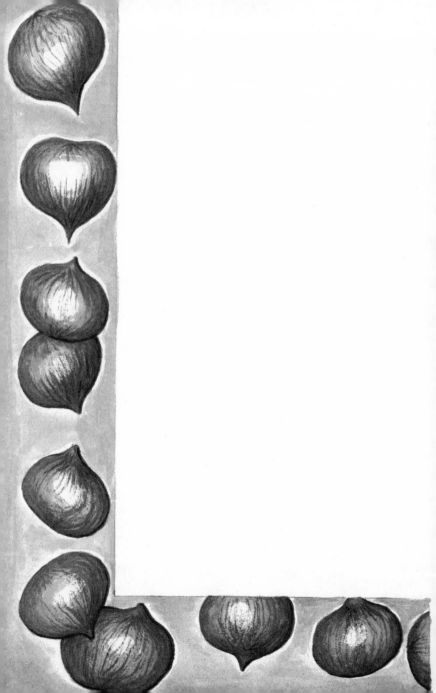

$\mathcal{S}$elect 25 large, ripe chestnuts and set them aside to soak in water. Later, peel them and simmer in milk, stirring constantly as they dissolve. Quickly remove the chestnut mixture from the heat, stirring constantly to ensure uniform consistency, and pour through a sieve.

If my mother saw me straining chestnuts with such pleasure, she would have a hard time believing it. She spent her whole life criticizing my lack of interest in cooking. Not that she was unfounded in her assessment, but you tell me, who would have a desire to cook after having spent two hours shredding chicken on her first day as a cook? That's just what happened once when my mother was

sick. At the ripe age of thirteen I thought
I could easily solve the world's problems,
especially where cooking was concerned.
But in order not to alarm my family too
much, I chose a very simple menu: noodle
soup and chicken tacos. Of course, if I had
known that the noodles had to be cut from
the dough *before* they were boiled and that
the chicken was supposed to be shredded
after it was cooked and not before, I would
have saved a lot of time and bother, but,
how was I to know?

I had a very happy childhood, playing
with my five brothers, far removed from the
kitchen. During that delightful period the
only thing that disturbed my tranquillity was
my obsessions. When I fell for a new game,
I really fell for it! I wouldn't stop until I had
mastered my technique and was the best in
the neighborhood. I fell for tops, I fell for
the yo-yo, I fell for marbles, I fell for roller

skates. The problems started when I fell for love. Oh! I practiced day and night. In no time, and after many boyfriends, there was no one knew how to hug, kiss, or caress like me. But curiously all the recognition and approval I obtained as champion in my previous activities vanished when I became a champion at love. My friends stopped speaking to me, not to mention my brothers, and my mother literally died of shame. Thank God, I say, because the poor woman didn't have to witness how I was mistreated. I couldn't even go to the corner without exposing myself to every sort of aggression and offense. So I decided to hide somewhere my brothers never went: the kitchen. And since I had nothing better to do, I fell for cooking. It took no time to master the arts of frying, beating, peeling, chopping, boiling, and browning all kinds of food. It was simply a matter of applying skills I had already

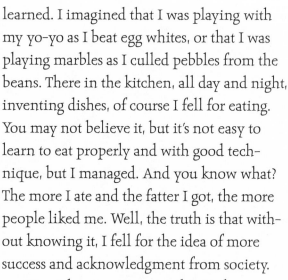

learned. I imagined that I was playing with my yo-yo as I beat egg whites, or that I was playing marbles as I culled pebbles from the beans. There in the kitchen, all day and night, inventing dishes, of course I fell for eating. You may not believe it, but it's not easy to learn to eat properly and with good technique, but I managed. And you know what? The more I ate and the fatter I got, the more people liked me. Well, the truth is that without knowing it, I fell for the idea of more success and acknowledgment from society.

Now I have a restaurant that is always crowded. All my ex-boyfriends come with their families and, because of my immense size, no one feels jealous of me, "fatty Pérez." I'm the favorite aunt and my whole family comes to eat as much as they can. I am, finally, the fattest millionaire in the country. So, why shouldn't I be happy to cook? And since I'm not an egotist, I am going to finish telling you the secrets of the dessert that has brought me the most fame: chestnut soufflé.

In a deep casserole, mix two ounces of fresh butter, a quart of boiled milk, and two tablespoons of flour until the flour is perfectly dissolved and blended. Separately, beat together an egg and one-half cup of powdered sugar. When the sugar is dissolved, add six yolks, the chestnut puree, and the flour and milk mixture. After mixing everything thoroughly, add six egg whites beaten to a firm peak. Then grease a baking pan with butter, pour in the mixture, and heat over a water bath until firm. That's all—just enjoy without any guilt. After all, you've seen that becoming terribly fat is not the end of the world; in fact, just the opposite, it could be the beginning of a whole new life.

Cooking with Chiles

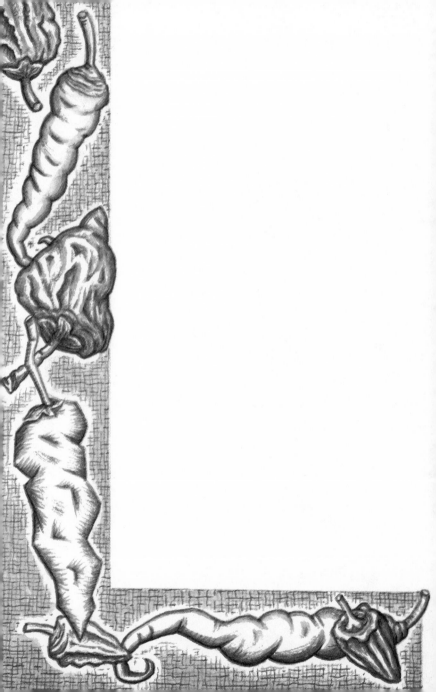

What Mexican hasn't eaten *chile?* Who hasn't gotten his fingers covered in *chile* juice? Who hasn't run the risk of smuggling a jar of *mole* or pickled *chiles* in his suitcase in hopes of continuing to enjoy the pleasure that *chile* gives its addicts? Who can remember the first time he felt his tongue burn, his forehead began to sweat, tears formed in his eyes, and his nose ran from eating *chiles?* No doubt it is very difficult to remember precisely because the *chile* is part of the ancestral memory of Mexicans and has been with us from time immemorial.

We know from the testimony of journalists that our indigenous forefathers ate *tortillas* and *tamales,* chickens and quails

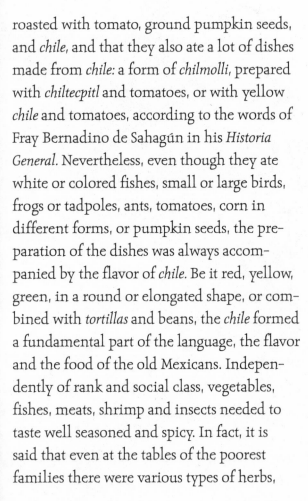

roasted with tomato, ground pumpkin seeds, and *chile*, and that they also ate a lot of dishes made from *chile:* a form of *chilmolli*, prepared with *chiltecpitl* and tomatoes, or with yellow *chile* and tomatoes, according to the words of Fray Bernadino de Sahagún in his *Historia General.* Nevertheless, even though they ate white or colored fishes, small or large birds, frogs or tadpoles, ants, tomatoes, corn in different forms, or pumpkin seeds, the preparation of the dishes was always accompanied by the flavor of *chile.* Be it red, yellow, green, in a round or elongated shape, or combined with *tortillas* and beans, the *chile* formed a fundamental part of the language, the flavor and the food of the old Mexicans. Independently of rank and social class, vegetables, fishes, meats, shrimp and insects needed to taste well seasoned and spicy. In fact, it is said that even at the tables of the poorest families there were various types of herbs,

nopal cactus, beans, tomatoes, and inevitably a portion of *chile*.

The act of eating transcended the limits of the home and overflowed into the streets and markets. We know that in the *plazas*, for example, *tortillas, tamales, atole*, dishes of meat with *chile* and tomato, *mole, chilaquiles, chilmoles, pozole*, and stews of *nenepile* or *mesclapiques* were sold. It wasn't strange for travelers to carry pine nuts or sweet potato candies, roasted ears of corn, *jícama*, or some other fruit of the season generously covered with *chile*. At the same time, since those times, rural people have maintained in their diet foods for their arduous labors beneath the sun, and among these the *chile* was never absent.

The *chile* was also used in the practicing of magic and spell casting. The varieties with elongated shapes were associated with the masculine figure and the wider, rounder

ones with the feminine. They were used to cleanse or as offerings so the good spirits could enjoy their benefits. They were burned to ward off evil spirits. They were used in rituals of thanksgiving, in ceremonies to deities of different orders and as medicinal plants. Because of their purging, disinfecting, and purifying properties they were used as poultices to alleviate swelling, or to cauterize, or as a pomade to cure stains on the skin, or even to facilitate the difficulties of birth and nursing.

Since remotest times there has not been an activity, public or private, profane or sacred, in Mexico where the presence of the *chile* has not been evident. Like a good guardian angel, it accompanies us always and does not forsake us night or day, in sickness or in health, in wealth or in poverty. Its influence in every area of our daily life is so powerful that it has survived the passage of time and all kinds of culinary influence. And so we modern Mexicans find ourselves continuing to eat exactly as our ancestors did, and each new food that has been included in our diet, we have made our own through the *chile*. From *bacalao* to hot dogs and hamburgers. Not only that, but we have also exported the *chile* to other cultures, and now there is talk of including the *chile* in the astronaut's diet.

A food staple, the *chile* has also invaded other orbits of our experience. It has become part of colloquial speech and has given a unique color to the expression of Spanish that is spoken in Mexico. Its use in speech is as diverse as its varieties and colors. It has meanings that range from clear and precise to vaguely implied and picaresque: *estar enchilado* (to be furious—a male); *estar enchilada* (to be furious—a female); *enchilarse* (to cover oneself—that is, one's fingers—with *chile*);

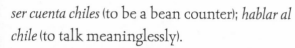

ser cuenta chiles (to be a bean counter); *hablar al chile* (to talk meaninglessly).

The *chile*, then, forms a vital part of our daily alimentation, and there is no table on which it doesn't play a primary importance because its flavor is carried in our memory and in our blood, and its spiciness flows in our veins.

If one is what he eats, with whom he eats it, and how he eats it, then we can conclude that we Mexicans are children of corn, but we were formed of *chile*. I wonder whether the gods created us together or separately, and if the latter, which came first, man or the *chile*.

Lowfat Mayonnaise

~~~~~~

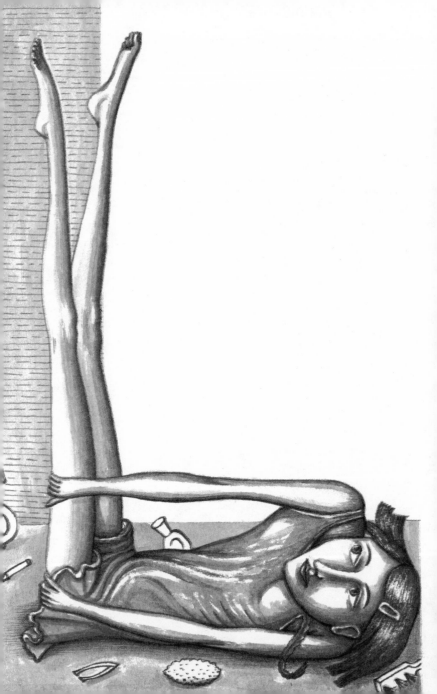

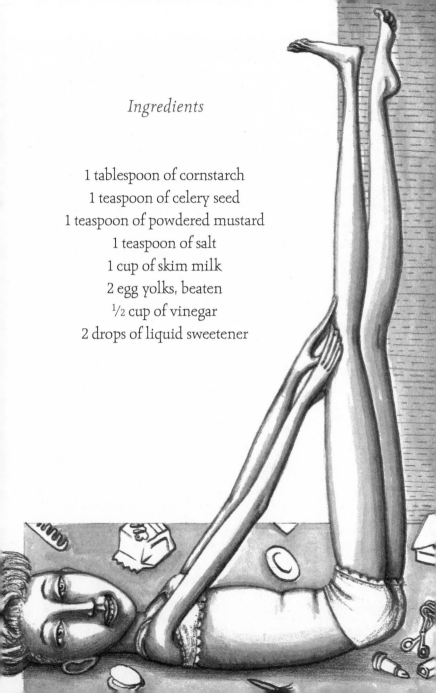

Ingredients

1 tablespoon of cornstarch
1 teaspoon of celery seed
1 teaspoon of powdered mustard
1 teaspoon of salt
1 cup of skim milk
2 egg yolks, beaten
½ cup of vinegar
2 drops of liquid sweetener

How far I am from the land where I was born,

immense nostalgia invades my thoughts,

and upon seeing me so alone and sad,

the leaf on the wind

would want to cry, would want to die

from compassion.

Oh, Land of the sun! I dream of seeing you, now that I find myself so far from you, shopping in a foreign supermarket. Everything is so coldly organized, sterile, functional that I am horrified. I ask myself what the hidden reason is behind this system of shopping. It seems that presenting food products in this manner has the objective of numbing our will and happiness. Upon seeing carrots, corn, lettuce, even *cilantro*, disguised to appear real even though they've been frozen for months, one feels that it's all part of a big set for an American movie. It's as if we are part of a huge superproduction in which we act as if we are choosing, buying, and eating these foods, but everything is simulated. In Mexico I am accustomed to going to the market every day, chatting with the merchants, tasting bites of fruit (real fruit) at each stand, running into my neighbors and talking to them among the magical smells and colors that are only found there. I am, essentially, accustomed to life.

I cannot find myself in these surroundings. I am losing my natural happiness. The only thing that cheers me up a little is eating chocolate doughnuts all day, but the bad part is that they have made me a little fat, and since fat women don't fit in American superproductions—you never see them on the screen, they just don't exist—so here I am buying the ingredients to make lowfat mayonnaise. To make it, you mix the cornstarch, celery seeds, mustard, and salt in a thick casserole. A little at a time, you add the skim milk and heat it over a low flame, constantly stirring until the mixture thickens. Cook for

two minutes, then remove it from the heat.
Once it has cooled a little, you add the egg
yolks and cook for another three minutes.
Remove it from the heat again and stir in the
vinegar and sweetener. Refrigerate before
serving. The recipe yields a cup and a quarter
and has only fifteen calories per tablespoon.
Can you believe it? Only fifteen calories per
tablespoon! When I finished the mayonnaise
and was ready to put it on a delicious salad,
I took out my calculator to add up the calories that I was going to eat and started to cry.
I took my plate back to the kitchen and went
to bed with a box of chocolate doughnuts
under my arm.

Apolonio

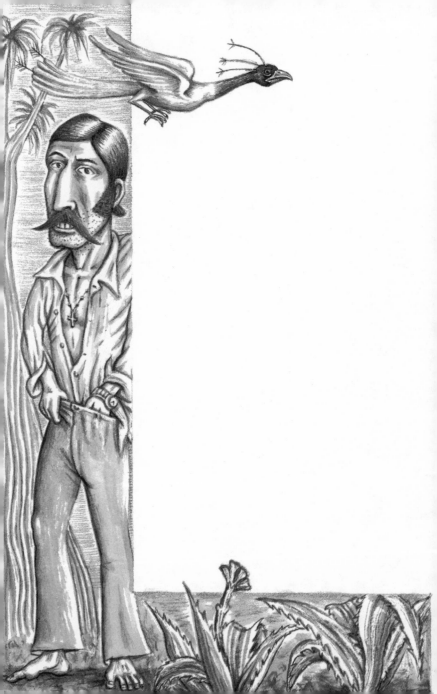

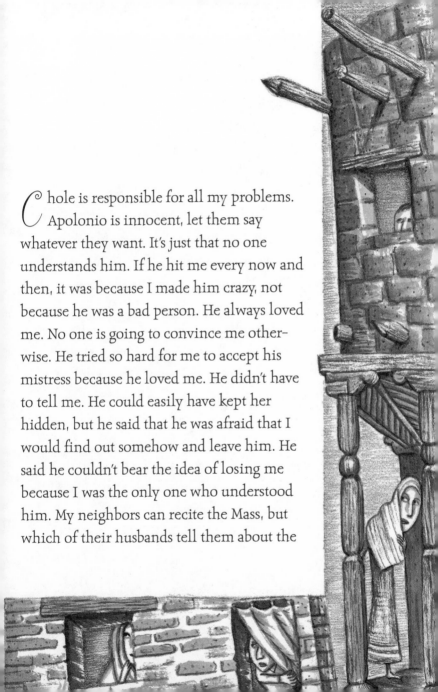

Chole is responsible for all my problems. Apolonio is innocent, let them say whatever they want. It's just that no one understands him. If he hit me every now and then, it was because I made him crazy, not because he was a bad person. He always loved me. No one is going to convince me otherwise. He tried so hard for me to accept his mistress because he loved me. He didn't have to tell me. He could easily have kept her hidden, but he said that he was afraid that I would find out somehow and leave him. He said he couldn't bear the idea of losing me because I was the only one who understood him. My neighbors can recite the Mass, but which of their husbands tell them about the string of lovers he has scattered around town? None! No, my Apolonio is the only honest one. The only one who takes care of me. The only one who worries about me. With all this about AIDS, it is very dangerous for husbands to be sleeping around, so instead of being with a lot of different women, he has decided to sacrifice himself and have only one lover. That way he won't risk infecting me with the disease. That is real love! What do my neighbors know anyway?!

Well, I have to acknowledge that at first it was difficult even for me to understand it. In fact, I originally told him no. Adela, my friend's daughter, was much younger than I was, and I was very afraid that Apolonio would prefer her to me. But my "Apo" convinced me that would never happen, that Adela didn't really matter to him. He said he had to take advantage of his last years of active manhood, because later he wouldn't be

133

able to. I asked him why he didn't take advantage of them with me and he explained, until I understood, that he couldn't, that it was one of the problems men had that women would never be able to understand. There was nothing exciting about sleeping with me; I was his wife and he could have me whenever he wanted. What he needed was to be able to prove that he could still seduce young women. If he couldn't, he would be traumatized, he would develop a complex, and then he wouldn't even be able to perform his duties with me. That is what really scared me.

I told him it was all right, I accepted that he had a mistress. Then he took me to speak with Adela, because Adelita had known me since she was a little girl and she felt very embarrassed and wanted to hear from my own mouth that I gave her permission to be Apolonio's mistress. She explained that she wasn't going to stay with him. She only wanted to help our marriage and she said that it was better for Apolonio to sleep with her and not just anyone who might have an interest in taking him away from me. I thanked her for her thoughtfulness and I think I even blessed her. In truth, I was thankful because she, too, was sacrificing herself for me.

Adela, with her youth, could easily have married and had children and instead she was willing to be Apolonio's steady mistress just because she was such a nice person.

Well, supposedly, I should have been very calm about all this. She came to the house; we spoke for a long time and cleared up everything. Schedules, visiting days, etc. Everything was under control. Apolonio was going to keep the peace and everyone would be happy. I don't know why I was still so sad.

When I knew Apolonio was with Adela I couldn't sleep. I spent the whole night imagining what they were doing. It didn't take a lot of imagination to figure out. I knew it, period. I couldn't stop feeling tormented. The worst part was that I had to pretend to be asleep when he came home so he wouldn't feel badly.

He didn't deserve that. He made me see that one day when he came home and found me awake. He was furious. He told me that I was a blackmailer, that I wouldn't let him enjoy himself in peace, that he had already given me proof of his love, and I was repaying him by spying on him and torturing him with my crying and my fears that he would never come back. Hadn't he always come back? Well, he was right; he came at five or six in the morning, but he always came back.

I had no reason to worry. I should have been happier than ever and only God knows why I wasn't! What's more, I began to grow sick of Apolonio's bursts of anger. It made me mad to see him buy Adela things he had never bought me. To stand by when he took her out to dance, and never took me dancing. Not even on my birthday when Celia Cruz was performing and I begged him to take me! My eyes turned yellow, my liver swelled, my breath became poisonous, and my skin developed spots from the rage I felt. That's when Chole told me that the best remedy in these cases was to put a handful of her special herbs in a liter of *tequila* and drink a shot while fasting. The *tequila* with the herbs draws out bile and removes anger from the body. I practically ran to the corner store, where I bought a bottle of *tequila* from don Pedro and added the herbs. The next morning I drank it and it worked very well.

Not only did I feel relieved inside, but I felt happier than I had been in many days. As time passed, the effects of the remedy increased. Apolonio, upon seeing

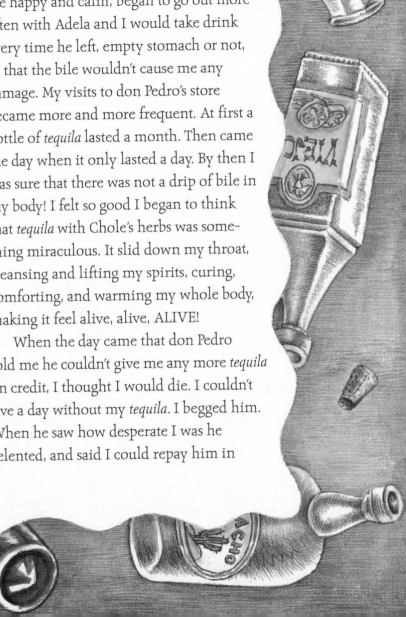

me happy and calm, began to go out more often with Adela and I would take drink every time he left, empty stomach or not, so that the bile wouldn't cause me any damage. My visits to don Pedro's store became more and more frequent. At first a bottle of *tequila* lasted a month. Then came the day when it only lasted a day. By then I was sure that there was not a drip of bile in my body! I felt so good I began to think that *tequila* with Chole's herbs was something miraculous. It slid down my throat, cleansing and lifting my spirits, curing, comforting, and warming my whole body, making it feel alive, alive, ALIVE!

When the day came that don Pedro told me he couldn't give me any more *tequila* on credit, I thought I would die. I couldn't live a day without my *tequila*. I begged him. When he saw how desperate I was he relented, and said I could repay him in another way. The poor man had always been attracted to me anyway. The pure truth is that with so much heat in my body I was eager too, and so Apolonio found us right there on the counter giving free rein to our pleasure.

Apolonio left me for being a drunk and a whore. Now he lives with Adela. And I am completely lost. All because of stupid Chole and her remedies!

Rosa Mexicano

Josefina Howard and I, apart from having a great friendship, share the same nationality. You might ask how this is so since she's not Mexican, but I would tell you that it doesn't matter in the least. One is what she eats, with whom she eats it, and how she eats it. Nationality is not determined by the place where one is born, but rather by the flavors and smells that accompany us from childhood. Nationality has to do with the Earth, but nothing to do with that poor idea of a territorial demarcation; it's something much more profound. It has to do with the products that the Earth provides, with its chemistry and its effects on our organisms. The biological compounds that we eat penetrate the

DNA of our cells and impregnate it with the most intimate flavors. They're absorbed into the deepest corners of our subconscious where our memories nest and roost forever in our minds.

Are only those people who were born in Mexico and who grew up eating *tortillas* Mexican? No, of course not. There are exceptional beings who are capable of arriving in an unknown city and, like children, let themselves be nurtured by cultures which are not theirs by birth. This is the case with Josefina. Her universal nature has allowed her to open herself to the world of smells and flavors of a Mexico that she made her own, and which responded to her by adopting her as a legitimate daughter.

The fraternity of the cooking stove is one of the strongest. When one enters a place and recognizes the smells that emanate from a pot of beans, from some freshly made *tortillas*, or from a simple *guacamole*, one knows that she is stepping on a tiny piece of Mexican soil. This was my experience the first time I entered Josefina's restaurant, Rosa Mexicano. I was immediately transported to Mexico, to Mexican cooking. To cooking with passion. Cooking that Josefina has dedicated herself to revealing and officiating over. Josefina, like any other Mexicana who is proud of being one, traveled abroad with her ration of *chiles* and her homemade *tortillas* to feed her nostalgia. Not only that, but driven by her desire to share the richness of the flavors of our cooking with everyone else, she took a chance on setting up a restaurant in the heart of Manhattan. In the book, *Rosa Mexicano*, one can enjoy dishes that range from the most sophisticated to the simplest, from the most universal to the most innovative.

In this book Josefina not only generously shares her recipes and her family's history in the most delicious manner, but she also allows us to travel pleasurably through the infinite possibilities and combinations that our culinary culture offers.

Josefina's lesson to us is one of solidarity and understanding among people. Only when one embraces this kind of solidarity is it possible to share cooking stoves, meals, happiness, and troubles. Happiness, at parties and in daily life. Troubles, at difficult and painful times of death and loss. Through this solidarity we are able to become one with the whole world, and share with one another that which makes us human and gives us a heritage born of the infinite inheritance of past flavors and smells, which ultimately means that we all share in the universality of food. So then, dear friends, let's bring together our glasses of *tequila* and toast Mexican food, *Rosa Mexicano*, and Josefina, la Mexicana.

Mother-Witch

One of the stories that terrorized me most as a child was the one about the witch that sucked children's blood. I saw the whole thing in my mind's eye in vivid detail. The witch capturing the child, the sucking of blood, the child's lifeless eyes, the mother's cries when she discovers the child's dead body, and especially the yellow color of the dead child's skin. I had trouble sleeping at night, and my back had to be pressed tightly against the wall to protect me from an attack from the rear.

It took me several years to realize that the real danger wasn't outside the house but inside it. And that the blood sucking wasn't a metaphor, since in addition to mothers and witches there are mother-witches in the world, a type of highly dangerous human that has the power to suck the life from its offspring. Why are these beings so dangerous? Because they have the appearance of a plain, simple mother, and they can even show affection, but at the same time they have a high capacity for manipulation; they control the will of their children and are able to bind their children's hands and mouths—the only elements that represent the expression of their individual creation and thought.

The binding of hands can occur in two ways: first, by forcing the child to behave through light pressure such as hitting, threatening, or blackmailing him, and second, by preventing the child's hands from following his individual impulses. So that, bound to obey, the hands lose their capacity for decision making and become simple objects of someone else's desire, instruments of the powerful will of the mother-witch.

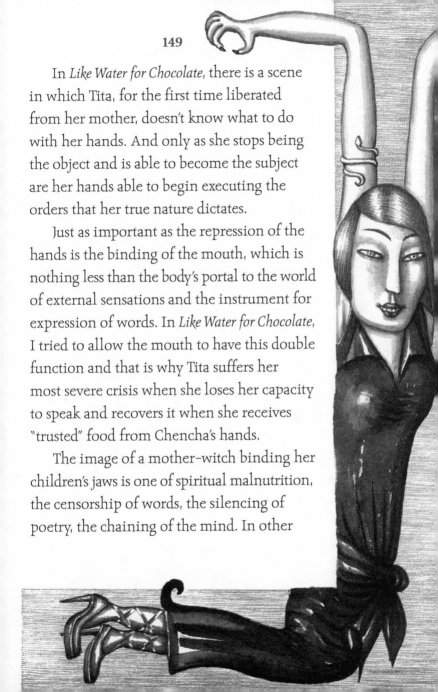

In *Like Water for Chocolate*, there is a scene in which Tita, for the first time liberated from her mother, doesn't know what to do with her hands. And only as she stops being the object and is able to become the subject are her hands able to begin executing the orders that her true nature dictates.

Just as important as the repression of the hands is the binding of the mouth, which is nothing less than the body's portal to the world of external sensations and the instrument for expression of words. In *Like Water for Chocolate*, I tried to allow the mouth to have this double function and that is why Tita suffers her most severe crisis when she loses her capacity to speak and recovers it when she receives "trusted" food from Chencha's hands.

The image of a mother-witch binding her children's jaws is one of spiritual malnutrition, the censorship of words, the silencing of poetry, the chaining of the mind. In other words it is the image of a true daughter of Coatlicue, the devourer, from Aztec history.

To help Tita confront her witch mother, I put a fairy godmother in her path. Nacha represents Tonantzin-Guadalupe, the good mother, the nurturing protector who uses food to liberate Tita's spirit, her sensuality, and all the desires she has silently accumulated. Nacha's presence is constant and appears when it is most needed. She is a powerful force tied to the earth and to life affirming traditions, the only force capable of defeating a mother-witch. Despite this, the struggle between the two is not an easy one since the mother-witch justifies her domination by citing tradition. Of course her concept of tradition is the opposite of the fairy god-mother's. It is not a good that belongs to us in a communal manner, it is not a moral value or a principle of collective memory, but rather a personal decision interpreted at the whim of the manipulator in question who pretends to be the defender of a truth that she herself represents: the youngest daughter must take care of her mother until she dies and must do this or that and must behave this way or that, etc.

The characteristics of the mother-witch are her dedication to control and her accumulated resentment. She does have real power, and it is based on her capacity to exercise authority without a masculine presence. She is a self-sufficient woman, without limits to control her capacity to devour. This cruel and despised "bloodsucker" has accumulated within herself the two symbolic forms of authority, the masculine and the feminine, converting herself in this manner into a power in disequilibrium, a force without a counterpart, a whimsical dictator, something in the manner of Mexico's political party, the PRI.

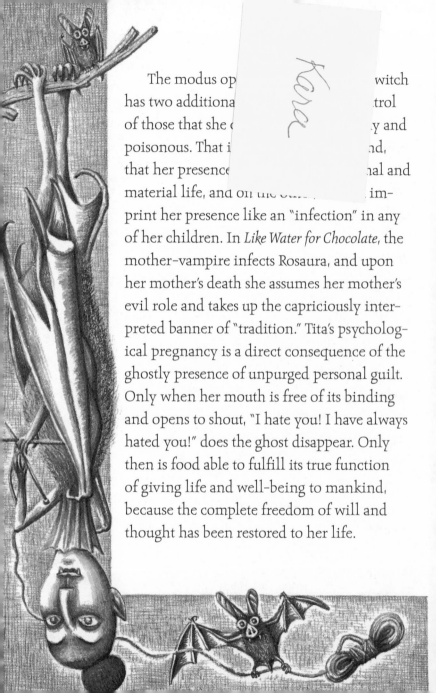

The modus op   witch
has two additiona   trol
of those that she   y and
poisonous. That i   d,
that her presence   al and
material life, and on the other   imprint her presence like an "infection" in any
of her children. In *Like Water for Chocolate*, the
mother-vampire infects Rosaura, and upon
her mother's death she assumes her mother's
evil role and takes up the capriciously interpreted banner of "tradition." Tita's psycholog-
ical pregnancy is a direct consequence of the
ghostly presence of unpurged personal guilt.
Only when her mouth is free of its binding
and opens to shout, "I hate you! I have always
hated you!" does the ghost disappear. Only
then is food able to fulfill its true function
of giving life and well-being to mankind,
because the complete freedom of will and
thought has been restored to her life.

Since confronting a mother-witch in *Like Water for Chocolate* and triumphing over her, not only have I given my mouth and hands the capacity to receive substances that feed my freedom, but I have also rid myself of the fear that a mother-witch would appear at night to suck my blood, and now I sleep much more soundly at night.

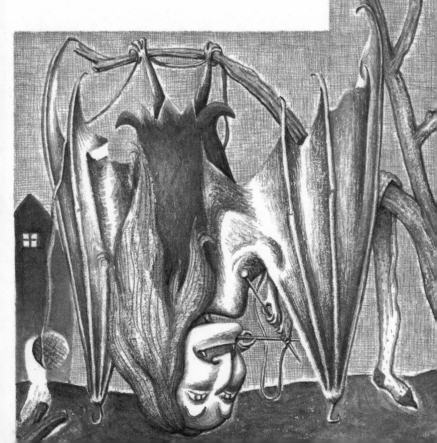

Credits

At the Hearth
Speech delivered at the National Museum of Anthropology
in Mexico City in January 1993 upon being recognized as
Woman of the Year, 1992.

God Is Above, the Devil, Below!
Published in the Mexican newspaper *Excelsior* on April 8, 1990.

Apple Soup
Published in *Vogue de México*. October 1989.

Between Two Fires
Prologue for the book *Appetite for Passion*.
Hyperion, New York, 1995.

Oaxacan Black Mole
Published in *Vogue de México*, May 1989.

Intimate Succulencies:
A Philosophic Treatise on Cooking
Speech given at the Guadalajara Book Fair, Mexico, 1990.

Manchamanteles
Published in *Vogue de México*, June 1989.

Introduction to Bread
Prologue for *The Secrets of Jesuit Breadmaking*, by Rick Curry. Harper Collins, New York, 1995.

Chestnut Soufflé
Published in *Vogue de México*, July 1989.

Cooking with Chiles
Prologue for the book *La Cocina del Chile*. Grupo Editorial Azabache, Mexico City, December 1993.

Lowfat Mayonnaise
Published in *Vogue de México*, November 1989.

Apolonio
Published in issue number 27 of the magazine *Artes de México*, *"El Tequila" Arte Tradicional de México*. December 1994.

Rosa Mexicano
Prologue for the book *Rosa Mexicano* by Josefina Howard. Viking Penguin, New York, 1998.

Mother-Witch
Speech to a group of psychoanalysts in Mexico City, December 4, 1997.